AWESOME
ANIMALS

First published in 2012 by
Miles Kelly Publishing Ltd
Harding's Barn, Bardfield End Green,
Thaxted, Essex, CM6 3PX, UK

Copyright © Miles Kelly Publishing Ltd 2011
This edition printed 2013

10 9 8 7 6 5 4 3 2

Publishing Director Belinda Gallagher
Creative Director Jo Cowan
Managing Editors Amanda Askew,
  Rosie McGuire
Managing Designer Simon Lee
Proofreaders Carly Blake, Claire Philip
Production Manager Elizabeth Collins
Image Manager Liberty Newton
Reprographics Stephan Davis
Assets Lorraine King

ISBN 978-1-84810-692-5

Printed in China

British Library Cataloguing-in-Publication Data
A catalogue record for this book is available
from the British Library

Made with paper from a sustainable forest

www.mileskelly.net
info@mileskelly.net

www.factsforprojects.com

ACKNOWLEDGMENTS

The publishers would like to thank the following sources for the use
of their photographs:

KEY Dreamstime=D, Fotolia=F, Frank Lane Picture Agency=FLPA, Getty
Images=GI, istockphoto.com=iS, Minden Pictures=MP, naturepl.com/Nature
Picture Library=NPL, Photolibrary=P, Shutterstock=S
t=top, a=above, b=bottom/below, c=center, l=left, r=right, f=far, m=main,
bg=background

COVER worldswildlifewonders/S BACK COVER Animal/S 1 Karen Givens/S
2 Pedro Nogueira/S 3(bg) Rich Lindie/S (strip, left to right) Yaroslav/S,
Antoni Murcia/S, cbpix/S, Johan Swanepoel/S, Kitch Bain/S 4–5 Christian
Ziegler/MP/FLPA 6(t) Jurgen & Christine Sohns/FLPA, (b) Hugh
Lansdown/FLPA 7(t) Stephen Dalton/NPL, (c) Stephen Dalton/NHPA,
(b) Gisela Delpho/P 8(m) Jurgen & Christine Sohns/FLPA, (bl) Kim
Taylor/NPL 9(t) Stephen Dalton/NPL, (b) Hue Chee Kong/S 10–1(bg) Alex
Kuzovlev, (m) Reinhard Dirscherl/P 10(t) Natutik/S 11(t) Michael & Patricia
Fogden/MP/FLPA, (br) Malcolm Schuyl/FLPA 12–3(bg) S, (bullet holes)
Krisdog/D, (nails) dusan964/S, (wanted posters) Chyrko Olena/S, (keys)
Simon Bratt/S 12(tl) Konstantin Sutyagin/S, (tr) Fred Bavendam/MP/FLPA,
(bl) Frank Stober/Imagebroker/FLPA, (br) ZSSD/MP/FLPA, (br, bg) Kirsty
Pargeter/F 13(tl) Austin J Stevens/P, (tr) Norbert Wu/MP/FLPA,
(bl) Mitsuaki Iwago/MP/FLPA, (bl, bg) Triff/S, (br, handcuffs) Zsolt
Horvath/S, (br, badge) Peter Polak/S 14–5(m) Piotr Naskrecki/MP/FLPA,
(frame) Undergroundarts.co.uk/S 14(l) Piotr Naskrecki/MP/FLPA, (b) Mark
Payne-Gill/NPL, (b, frame) Robert Adrian Hillman/S 15(t) S & D & K
Maslowski/FLPA, (b) Ron Austing/FLPA 16–7(bg) Gudrun Muenz/S,
(labels) Picsfive/S, (balloons) Michael C. Gray/S, (streamers) hans.slegers
16(tl) Ariadne Van Zandbergen/FLPA, (cl) Milena_/S, (c) Manfred Kage/P,
(c, frame) Natalie-art/S, (br) Sherjaca/Shutterstock 17(tl) Eduardo Rivero/S,
(tl, frame) vector-RGB/S, (tr) laschi/S, (cl) Pete Oxford/NPL,
(cl, bg) LeonART/S, (cr) Eky Studio/S, (cr, frame) Nira/S, (b) Paul Kay/P,
(b, party hat) Stacy Barnett/S 18(m) Sea Pics, (b) Bruce Davidson/NPL
19(t) javarman/S, (cl) Ron O'Connor/NPL, (b) Paul Nicklen/GI
20–1(colored paper) Alexey Khromushin/F, (frame) Picsfive/S, (pins) Oleksii
Natykach/S, composite image: (hind legs) Steffen Foerster Photography/S,
(tail) NREY/S, (body) Eric Isselée/S, (front legs) Eric Isselée/S, (neck)

prapass/S, (ears) Johan Swanepoel/S 20(t) Dhoxax/S, (c) Mark Beckwith/S,
(b) Mogens Trolle/S, (paper) Milos Luzanin/S 21(tl) michael Sheehan/S,
(tr) BlueOrange Studio/S, (cl) Kjersti Joergensen/S, (cr) Ludmila Yilmaz/S,
(bl) Jurgen & Christine Sohns/FLPA, (br) Steffen Foerster Photography/S
22–3(tl) Aflo/NPL, (tc) pixelman/S, (tr) Villiers Steyn/S, (bl) Stephen
Bonk/S, (br) Neil Bowman/FLPA 24–5(bg) Lightspring/S, (c) Roger
Powell/NPL, (panels) tkemot, (stars) Tomasz Wojdyla 24(tl) Geoff
Simpson/NPL, (bl) Andy Rouse/NPL, (br) Tui De Roy/P 25(tl) Eric Isselée/S,
(tr) Dietmar Nill/NPL, (cr) Doug Allan/NPL, (br) Ed Reschke/P
26–7(bg, wood) Brian Weed/S, (bg, book) thumb/S, (doodles) Petr
Vaclavek/S, (c) Tyler Boyes/S, (bc) Danny Smythe/S 26(l) vilax/S,
(tr) Angelo Gandolfi/NPL, (b) Suzi Eszterhas/MP/FLPA 27(tl) Constantinos
Petrinos/NPL, (tr) Marie Read/NPL, (bl) Premaphotos/NPL, (br) Doug
Perrine/NPL, (acorns) dionisvera/S 28–9(m) Tan Hung Meng/S,
(leaves) maxstockphoto/S 28 Colin Marshall/FLPA, 29(t) S Charlie
Brown/FLPA, (b) Bruce Davidson/NPL 30–1(bg) Lasse Kristensen/S
30(tr) Katherine Feng/MP/FLPA, (c) Cathy Keifer/iS (b) ImageBroker/FLPA,
(bl) Cathy Keifer/F 31(t) Mitsuaki Iwago/MP/FLPA, (c) Donna Heatfield/S,
(b) Visuals Unlimited/NPL 32(m) Neale Cousland/S, (l) Vinicius
Tupinamba/S 33(tl) Johan Swanepoel/S, (tr) mike lane/Alamy, (cl) Joseph
DiGrazia/S, (cl, frame) Iwona Grodzka/S, (b) Kurt Madersbacher/P
34–5(medal) Fotocrisis/S 34(m) Gerry Ellis/MP/FLPA, (b) Flip De
Nooyer/FN/MP/FLPA 35(t) Johan Swanepoel/S, (b) Mike Parry/MP/FLPA
36–7(bg) Pete Oxford/NPL, (yellow leaf) Iurii Konoval/S, (green
leaf) maxstockphoto/S 36(tr) Staffan Widstrand/NPL, (bl) Thomas
Marent/MP/FLPA 37(t) Heidi & Hans-Juergen Koch/MP/FLPA, (c) Solvin
Zankl/NPL, (b) Gerry Ellis/MP/FLPA, (frames) PhotoHappiness/S
38–9(tc) Richard Fitzer/S, (tc, sign) Loskutnikov/S, (bc) Flip
Nicklin/MP/FLPA, (r) Anan Kaewkhammul/S, (boards) aborisov/S

All other photographs are from: Corel, digitalSTOCK, digitalvision,
Dreamstime.com, Fotolia.com, iStockphoto.com, John Foxx, PhotoAlto,
PhotoDisc, PhotoEssentials, PhotoPro, Stockbyte

Every effort has been made to acknowledge the source and copyright
holder of each picture. The publishers apologise for any unintentional
errors or omissions.

AWESOME
ANIMALS

Steve Parker

Consultant: Camilla de la Bedoyere

Miles Kelly

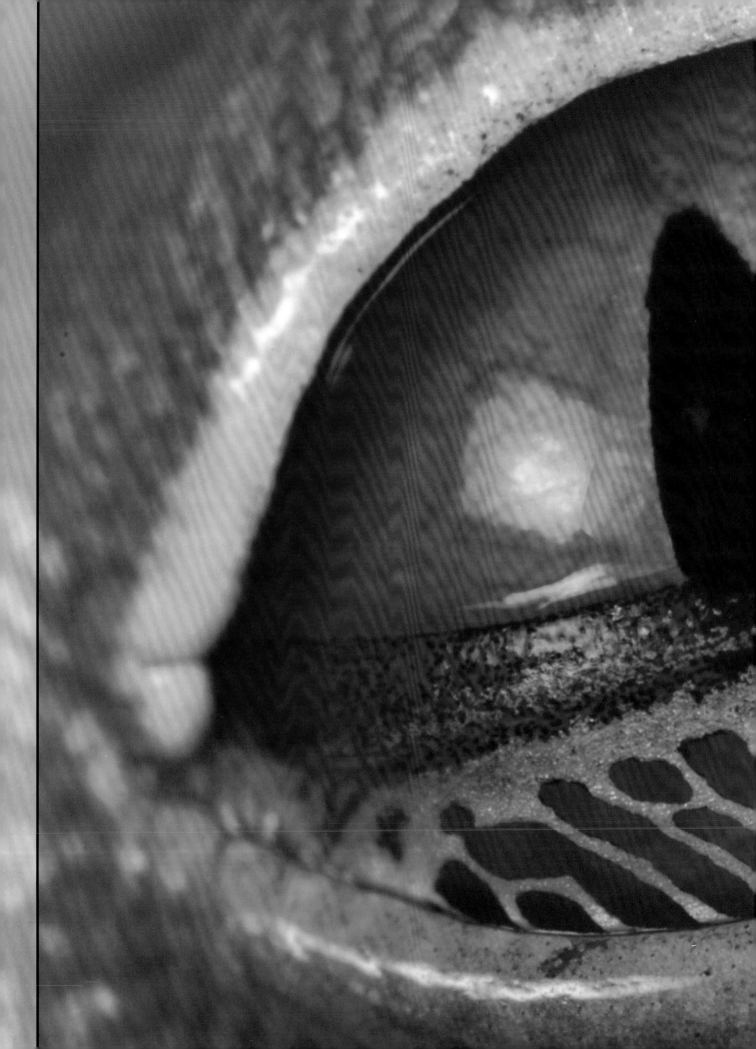

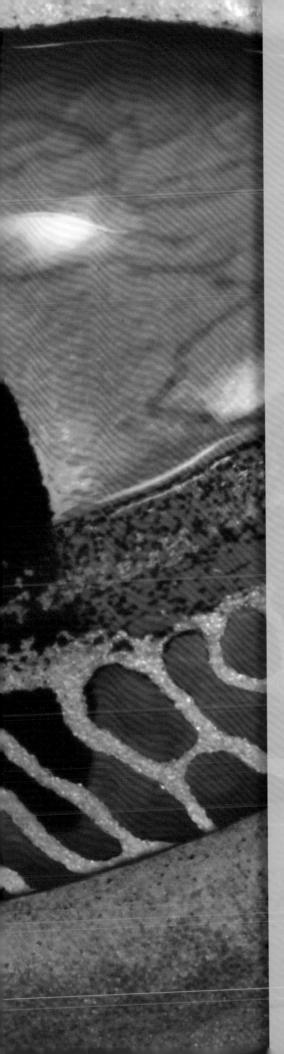

CONTENTS

◄ The red-eyed tree frog has a thin membrane that partly covers its brightly colored eye. This allows the frog to see while remaining camouflaged.

Unusual MOVES

All animals need to move to find food, seek shelter, escape enemies, and of course link up with breeding partners. Most creatures walk, run, fly, or swim, depending on their habitat, but some use unusual and unexpected ways of moving—such as flying with their feet!

Feet feats

From cheetahs and deer to ostriches and cockroaches, long, slim legs are a sure sign of speedy sprinters. There are many ways to get about on foot—kangaroos hop, grasshoppers leap, fleas jump, and some lizards and bugs even walk on water. However, few creatures are bipedal (move around regularly on two legs). A lizard may rear up briefly in fear, and an orangutan might amble along a branch, but only a select few—birds and humans—have the upright posture and delicate balance for bipedal walking.

▲ The sifaka, a large Madagascan lemur, holds out its arms for balance while it moves using short, sideways hops.

▲ The mudskipper uses its muscular armlike pectoral fins to haul its body across the tidal ooze. If in danger, this bizarre fish flips its whole body into the air to move to safety.

◀ Frogs usually use their webbed feet to provide a powerful push when swimming. However, the flying frog of Southeast Asia sails through the air using its webs like mini-parachutes to increase drag, slowing its descent.

Emergency aerobats

There's a massive difference between actual flying, like a bird, and a perilous leap into midair with just flaps of skin preventing a fatal plummet to the ground. "Flying" squirrels, lizards, frogs, and snakes don't actually fly, but glide. Their aerial ability is mainly used for emergencies. They create a broad surface, often by opening out flaps of skin, which encounters air resistance to slow their fall. A tilt or twist gives some control over direction, and a few bruises on landing are preferable to being gobbled up by a predator.

CLOCKED AT MORE THAN 65 MPH (105 KM/H), THE SAILFISH IS THE FASTEST SWIMMER IN THE WORLD.

▶ Using its partly webbed toes and fast strides, the basilisk lizard races on its hind legs across water—with no time to sink.

Water sports

Muscle-packed bodies and thrashing fins give fish speed—the fastest species, such as the sailfish, have stiff, narrow, crescent-shaped tails. However, fins are adaptable and can be used for out-of-water movement, too, such as in the goby and walking catfish. Bird wings are similar in shape to fins and some birds use them to thrust through water rather than air. Kingfishers and dippers can "swim" briefly, but penguins have given up air flight completely.

▲ The kingfisher, using its wings as both rudders and underwater brakes, stri...

COOL
Senses

All around are more light rays, sounds, and smells than humans could ever imagine. Animals of all kinds can tune into this abundance of sensations with their amazing supersenses. Often an animal is almost entirely dependent on just one dominant sense—block a bat's ears or an anteater's nostrils and they cannot survive.

▶ Giant anteaters sniff out their tiny quarry from more than 150 ft (45 m) away.

▼ The male cockchafer beetle's feathery antennae (feelers) detect scent particles, called pheromones, from females up to several miles away. These pheromone messages tell the male that the females are ready to mate.

Sniff, snort, snuffle

A polar bear can sniff out a seal carcass up to 4.5 mi (7 km) away, while a human would need to be within 300 ft (90 m) to detect even a trace of this rotting stench. Bears, wolves, and dogs far exceed a human's capacity because they have more than 200 million microscopic smell cells in their noses, compared to a human's five million. The sense of smell is not just for finding food. Without it, elephants would die of thirst, lions would not be able to mark their territory, and many moths and beetles could never detect scents released by potential mates that tell them they are ready to breed.

RHINO Sight estimated at five times poorer than a human's—it cannot distinguish between another rhino and a jeep at 300 ft (90 m) away. However, its sense of smell is ten times better than a human's.

EAGLE Sight is at least ten times better than a human's—it can see a rabbit more than 2 mi (3 km) away.

BAT Hearing can pick up vibrations ten times faster than a human—so it can hear a tiny gnat's flapping wings.

MOTH Sense of smell is more than 10,000 times more sensitive than a human's—it can scent nectar from a blossom that a human could not even see in daylight!

▲ A bat finds its way around using echolocation—it squeaks and then listens to the echoes to work out where objects in its path are. Large ears help a bat to gather these sounds. If a human's ears were relative in size to the long-eared bat's, they would be bigger than trashcan lids!

Hear, hear!

A noise that sounds quiet to a human might deafen an owl or a bat. They have far more microsensors in their ears, and they move their ears or head much more carefully to receive the maximum number of sound waves and pinpoint an object's position. Ears are not always on the head. Insects such as grasshoppers and crickets have them on their knees, and some fish "hear" with their swim bladders.

Seeing the invisible

Animal eyes can see infrared and ultraviolet light—both of which are outside the spectrum of light that is visible to humans. Insects in particular are highly tuned to these invisible wavelengths. To a bee, plain-looking petals are covered with ultraviolet lines that point to the sweet nectar inside. Some fish have an amazing sense of sight, too. Piranhas can see the warm, infrared glow of a mammal—then launch their mass attack.

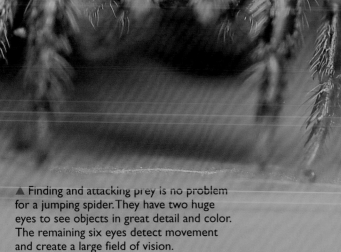

▲ Finding and attacking prey is no problem for a jumping spider. They have two huge eyes to see objects in great detail and color. The remaining six eyes detect movement and create a large field of vision.

The GROSS Factor

Animals have some disgusting habits. To deter predators, they spray vomit or excrement, spit saliva, and even squirt blood from open vessels. When it comes to feeding, they certainly have no manners—tearing at flesh and creating a bloody mess. Some animals even tuck into excrement for a tasty snack.

THE HORNED LIZARD SQUIRTS A BLOODY FLUID FROM ITS EYES— MORE THAN 5 FT (1.5 M)—AT A THREAT.

Disgusting defense

Vomit, slime, urine, droppings, spit, and pus can sting, cause infection, and create an off-putting stench. Some animals capitalize on this by using their bodily fluids to make enemies recoil and retreat. The innocent-looking sea cucumber throws up its super-sticky guts over an attacker, while several kinds of seabird projectile vomit more than 3 ft (1 m) at an enemy.

▼ The world's largest lizards have big appetites. Komodo dragons feast on a rotting dolphin carcass, enjoying the fatty blubber and the guts filled with semidigested fish. Male komodos can reach lengths of 10 ft (3 m).

Feeding frenzy

Even before a huge pile of food becomes available, predators and scavengers wait in the wings. A dying whale is tracked by sharks, orcas, and seabirds, while a sick elephant lures hyenas, jackals, and vultures. As soon as one plucks up the courage to move in for a mouthful, the rest rush to grab what they can. The feeding frenzy that follows is rough, gory, and urgent as they push and scrap to get the best share before it's all gone.

Messy breeders

Animal babies can be born in the most disgusting conditions. Some parasitic wasp grubs hatch in the guts of a caterpillar, and proceed to eat the host alive. Dung beetle grubs emerge from their eggs into balls of excrement. Surinam toad tadpoles develop inside their mother's back, under her skin. Other frogs whip up a foam using a cocktail of their saliva, skin slime, sperm fluid, and excrement, and lay their eggs here.

▼ A group of male gray foam-nest tree frogs cluster around one female and whip their bodily fluids into a froth, in which she deposits her spawn.

Nasty nourishment

Dung, droppings, and excrement might look and smell horrible. However, the digestion of most animals is not very efficient, so feces often still contain plenty of nutrients. Dung eaters usually like to get it while it's fresh, before molds, germs, and flies arrive to contaminate the rotting mass.

▲ This turkey vulture quickly devours fishy feces from a fur seal.

Wicked ASSASSINS

Natural born killers are feared for their deadly weapons. These fearsome animals mercilessly slay their prey with lethal teeth, claws, and fangs, devouring flesh, bones, and blood with ease—no morsel is spared.

Wolfie the Wolffish

Last seen in the waters of the Atlantic Ocean, the wolffish is 5 ft (1.5 m) long and can be recognized by its vast number of teeth. It has about 100 of them—fanglike at the front, broad for crushing at the back, and continuing into its throat. Its typical victims are shellfish, starfish, crabs, and urchins, which the wolffish crushes to death with great power.

WANTED

Terminator
the Alligator

This 15-ft- (4.6-m-) long 'gator is wanted for drowning prey by dragging it underwater. Victims include turtles, snakes, waterbirds, and mammals up to the size of deer. Beware—the alligator is armed and dangerous, with 50 cone-shaped teeth and amazingly strong jaw muscles. Do not approach.

WANTED
REWARD $2,000

JAWS
THE GRIZZLY BEAR

Towering up to 10 (3 m) tall, the grizzly i a formidable hunter Its weapons include powerful teeth and jaws, plate-sized paws, and curved claws. These features, combined with enormous weight, power, and stamina, mean that nothing is safe. The grizzly will attack anything up to the size of moose and never lets go.

FANG THE GABOON VIPER

The Gaboon viper is a massive 6 ft (2 m) long. Mice, rats, birds, and similar small creatures have been found dead, marked with puncture wounds. This cold-blooded killer strikes at lightning speed, using its long, foldout front fangs to stab the victim's flesh and inject deadly venom. It then waits for the victim to die of shock as the heart stops beating (cardiac arrest).

WANTED
DEAD OR ALIVE

Lurking in the shadows of the deep, the 11-ft- (3.5-m-) long sand tiger shark charges suddenly, taking its victim by surprise. Fish, squid, shellfish, and crabs have all suffered from this menace's slashing bite.

SMILER THE SAND TIGER SHARK

MOST WANTED

A master of stealth, this 8-ft- (2.4-m-) long assassin camouflages itself among the grass, stalking before the sudden rush of attack. Armed with huge canine teeth and slicing back teeth, victims are killed with a throat-crushing bite, before the lion tears its flesh apart using sharp, curved claws. An experienced killer, no "hit" is too big or small for this ferocious feline. Its kill list includes gazelles and antelope, as well as rats and beetles.

CLAWS THE LION

SHERIFF

BABOONS OFTEN KILL OTHER BABOONS TO BECOME THE BOSS OF THE TROOP.

Deadly
DEFENSE

The forest is nearly dark and almost quiet. A creature sneaks up on the juicy meal it has been tracking. It steadies itself, preparing to pounce... WOAH! Suddenly two huge eyes appear, glaring in the gloom. A big cat? A snake? An owl? No, they're eyespots (false eyes)—one of many animal self-defense tactics.

Terrible taste

Having horrible-tasting or poisonous flesh deters predators and works as a great group defense strategy. After biting one foul-tasting animal, a hunter learns to recognize its warning signs, such as colors and patterns, and stays away from all similar-looking prey.

◀ The African foam grasshopper shows its nasty taste by blowing noxious bubbles from tiny breathing holes, called spiracles, along its body.

Animal armor

Some creatures lack speed to escape enemies, or foul-tasting defenses to deter them. Instead they use simple physical protection. Tough-shelled animals include crabs, clams, and snails, as well as armadillos and pangolins. They simply shut up tight and wait for the danger to pass.

▶ The three-banded armadillo has bony plates within its skin, covered by outer scales of horny keratin. Its armor is so flexible that it can curl into a tight ball that will completely defeat predators.

◄ A rear view of the peacock katydid (a type of grasshopper) shows how its suddenly raised wings display enormous eyespots to startle a potential attacker.

PLAYING DEAD

When under threat, the Virginia opossum flops onto its side, puts out its tongue, leaks foul-smelling anal fluid, and emits a rotting stench. By acting "dead," no hunter will try to eat it.

Guns blazing

Camouflage is a great defense tactic. An animal that matches the background color of its habitat can just sit still and hope to go unnoticed. But what if it's spotted? The next tactic is to make a grand show of defense—rear up, look big, reveal your weapons, make a noise, wave and shake, and generally try to look as frightening and inedible as possible.

► If its disguise is rumbled, the dead-leaf mantis raises its body and extends its wings and fearsome, spiked, jackknife forelegs to appear super-fierce.

Young and Old

Why do elephants live longer than flies? These creatures are at two ends of a whole spectrum of life strategies. One is to develop slowly, and take great care of just a few young. The other is to live fast and die young, mating frequently and producing lots of offspring but providing no parental care.

4 MONTHS

Congratulations!

Labord's chameleon

Shortest-lived of any four-legged vertebrate, this lizard's life cycle is perfectly adapted to Madagascar's seasonal changes. It lives for a single year, spending eight months in an egg and just four months in its adult form.

1 DAY!

Have a Great Day!

happy birthday!

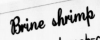

1 TODAY!

Brine shrimp

Old shrimps lay tough-cased eggs before their salt lake dries up for summer. When it starts to rain in fall, the eggs hatch, and the next generation begins to feed.

I AM 3 WEEKS OLD

Bee Happy!

Mayfly

The mayfly spends a year or two as an underwater nymph. Then it emerges, molts to reveal its wonderful wings, mates in midair, and dies—all within 24 hours.

Worker honeybee

Day after day of nonstop toil means the worker honeybee's body suffers immense wear and tear. The egg-laying queen might make it to five years old.

50!

Macaw

Several parrot species may reach the half-century mark. Intelligence—along with their powerful beaks and claws—help these birds to survive.

BIRTHDAY GREETINGS!

70 Today

Elephant

Size and power provide protection against lions and other foes, and family ties mean younger and more vulnerable members of the herd are well-guarded by the females of the group.

175

giant birthday!

Giant tortoise

Life in the slow lane, with a reptile's unhurried body chemistry, plentiful food, few natural predators, and a thick, protective shell, is a great recipe for reaching a great age.

220 TODAY

220

HAPPY BIRTHDAY

Koi carp

These precious and pampered ornamental fish are popular pets because they reach a great age, in addition to their beautiful coloration.

Quahog clam

This shellfish holds the record for the longest life (and perhaps the most boring—it spends all of its many days lying on the dark seabed).

400 TODAY!

Dinner TIME

In the wild, animals rarely know where their next meal is coming from, so any snack is greedily gobbled up. If a glut of food appears, some species will eat until they are almost bursting—the opportunity to devour their fill may not come again.

▶ The Bryde's whale spends all day filtering tiny creatures such as krill and small fish from the water. Its daily diet can weigh 3 tons—equivalent to the amount of food eaten by a human over a period of seven or eight years.

▼ This African bullfrog has no teeth and cannot tear up or chew its mouse victim. Instead, frogs and toads feed by stretching their head-wide mouths and gulping prey whole.

Down in one

The bodies of many creatures are adapted for eating huge amounts in a single feeding session. Features range from a stretchy stomach to a dislocating jaw. With scavengers and enemies lurking everywhere, fast food is best—rapid gulps or the all-in-one swallow. After gorging their fill, these gluttons can hide away from danger while they digest.

Leave it in the larder

Some animals store excess food for later, to avoid waste and prepare for periods when food is scarce. Squirrels bury nuts, crocodiles wedge gazelles beneath underwater rocks, and tigers scrape leaves and soil over deer carcasses. These clever methods mean these creatures are less likely to die of starvation when times are hard.

▶ The leopard can haul a kill three times its own weight up into a tree, away from scavengers such as jackals.

▼ These white-backed vultures rush to peck the juiciest morsels from a dead giraffe, before a pack of hyenas arrive on the scene.

Scavenger hunt

Old meat is still a valuable source of nourishment, so a large carcass attracts a multitude of scavengers. The first (airborne vultures) and the fiercest (hyena clans) get the richest pickings. Lesser scavengers such as jackals soon follow.

Bite to kill

Any predator must make careful decisions about which prey to tackle, and how. If an animal has just eaten, it may feel full and sluggish, and this might put it off tackling another large victim. A predator will also assess the fitness of potential prey—is it strong and healthy, or (preferably) too young, old, or sick, for its defenses to prove a problem? The attack itself must be swift and decisive, since in the wild even a slight injury makes a hunter far less capable.

▶ After a lightning, twist-and-turn chase, the leopard seal strikes with its viciously sharp canine teeth. The seal moves in as the penguin weakens, and chomps away at the fatty blubber and tasty flesh.

The Perfect Animal?

Every species is superbly adapted to its habitat and way of life. But some creatures' features are super-adapted, compared to other, similar animals. If we could bring together all these extreme adaptations into one combi-creature, surely it would instantly be crowned king of the animal kingdom?

Ringtailed lemur's TAIL

Not only an excellent balance aid, the lemur's tail is used to convey signals about mood and intention. The male sprays a nasty scent on its own tail and waves it at opponents to mark its territory. The tail also indicates an individual's rank within the group, and attracts a mate.

Cheetah's BODY

Slim and streamlined, the fastest land animal's body is lithe yet muscular and flexible, and ideal for out-sprinting prey.

Gerenuk's HIND LEGS

Slim and strong, this antelope rears up on its hind legs to reach juicy leaves in tall trees—food that few other animals can reach.

Elephant's EARS
Not only brilliant for catching faint sounds, the world's biggest ears can flap both to lose internal heat and to fan cooling air over the body.

Tarsier's EYES
The tarsier hunts by grabbing passing moths and bats, so its massive eyes have a fabulous ability to follow fast motion, as well as superb vision even on the darkest nights.

Tiger's MOUTH
Huge, sharp teeth and one of the biggest, strongest bites of any land animal ensures that any victim is fatally wounded in an instant.

Proboscis monkey's NOSE
Long and drooping, this remarkable nose amplifies hoots and calls, and also offers a superior sense of smell compared to other monkey species.

Giraffe's NECK
As well as reaching far higher food than any other ground-bound animal, a giraffe's excellent vantage point gives it an all-round aerial view—so it can spot approaching predators from a long way off.

Kangaroo's LEGS
The kangaroo's hind legs offer an energy-efficient, bouncing gait, with the added extra of huge leaps 26 ft (8 m) long and 13 ft (4 m) high.

The natural world is both nice and nasty, when animals of two different species live together in a symbiotic relationship. Here, both partners help each other in some way for mutual benefit.

▶ As the clownfish swims around the anemone, water circulation increases, which helps the anemone to breathe.

Best of friends

Sea anemones and clownfish work together in harmony. Although anemones feed by paralyzing small fish with their stinging tentacles, the clownfish's slimy coating resists the venom. The anemone recognizes this and rarely attempts to attack. In return for this safe haven, the clownfish eats debris and pests among the tentacles to keep the anemone clean. The anemone also scares off animals that may prey on clownfish, while the clownfish lures in other fish to be eaten by the anemone.

▶ Ants crowd around the aphids and "milk" them so they secrete sweet, sugar-rich honeydew.

Buddies vs Baddies

Sometimes partnerships are horribly one-sided. One benefits, while the other gets hurt—the parasite-host situation. But being a parasite is a balancing act. If you are too successful, all your hosts die out and you have nowhere to live and nothing to eat.

Eaten alive

Some of the nastiest parasites are small wasps that lay their eggs in living caterpillars and other larvae. The wasp stings and paralyzes the caterpillar, then deposits its eggs inside the host's body. The wasp grubs hatch and proceed to eat the helpless host bit by bit.

▼ This tomato hornworm caterpillar is covered with parasitic wasp eggs. Its death will be slow as the hatched grubs chomp away until all that's left is an empty skin.

Protection for food

Aphids (greenfly and blackfly) are tiny, soft, and defenseless—except when they are in the care of an ant colony. While the aphids feed on plant sap with their sucking mouthparts, ants from a nearby nest patrol the region and keep away aphid enemies, such as ladybugs. In return for their protection, the ants feed on a sugary liquid, called honeydew, produced by the aphids.

▼ This impala is being "cleaned" by red-billed oxpeckers. Although they get rid of pests, oxpeckers may also peck at their host's skin, keeping wounds open—making this bird both a helper and a parasite.

A quick cleanup

The oxpecker doesn't only peck oxen—it may debug antelope, gazelles, giraffes, zebras, rhinos... as well as many more. The bird feeds on pests, such as lice, fleas, and ticks, especially in hard-to-reach places, as well as blood from any open wounds.

▶ This common cuckoo fledgling dwarfs its eager dunnock foster parent. The dunnock's instinct to feed its young is so strong, it fails to recognize that this giant youngster is an imposter.

Crafty cuckoo

A brood parasite takes advantage of other animals at breeding time, using them to raise its own offspring. The female cuckoo lays her egg in another bird's nest. The chick hatches, pushes out the other eggs, and demands food from its new parents. Other brood parasites include cowbirds, whydahs, and honeyguides.

SHOWTIME
Spectacular!

Rivals for attention

Impressing partners is only a part of courtship. Animals may also have to compete with rivals who want to get in on the action and steal their partner.

Most creatures spend their time keeping a low profile, trying to stay unnoticed by predators. But there are times when an animal needs to make itself known, showing off any special features, either to attract a mate or to discourage a rival or enemy from approaching.

FLICKER, FLASH
The female **glowworm** is actually a wingless beetle and glows to attract a winged male for mating.

DRESS UP
A male **ruff** erects his beautiful soft collar of pale feathers as he struts and calls when breeding.

KICK, PUNCH
A female **hare** plays hard to get as she "boxes" with a male to test his health, speed, reactions, and vigor.

BLOW UP
A male **greater frigate** stretches his gular (throat) pouch to show his potential as a mating partner.

Courting couples

Animal courtship is not just a quick flirt for fun—it's a serious test. Each partner checks the other is the correct species, strong and healthy, and will pass on good genes to any offspring.

FAN OUT
A **peacock** fans out his shimmering, green tail to impress a peahen. The brighter the colors, the more attractive his tail appears.

FEED ME
A **European bee-eater** pair give each other food morsels as they flutter like butterflies when courting.

PUFF OUT
The male **hooded seal** impresses potential partners by inflating a balloon of skin out of its nose.

FLAG UP
A courting male **anole lizard** flicks out his colorful throat fan, or dewlap, to attract a mate.

Bright SPARKS

Q: What do chimps, dolphins, octopuses, elephants, parrots, dogs, and monkeys have in common?

A: They are some of the animal world's smartest cookies. Their range of talents—including tool use, problem solving, and teamwork—make them top of the class.

Using tools

Many animals have developed incredible techniques to obtain food otherwise unattainable for them. The Egyptian vulture uses a stone as a hammer to crack a tough egg, while the woodpecker finch extracts grubs from tree holes with a cactus spine. The master is the chimp—it not only uses tools, but also modifies them. For example, it chews the end of its termite "fishing stick" to make it sleeker and easier to poke into the mound.

The Egyptian vulture drops a stone onto an ostrich egg to break it open and feed on the nutritious contents.

1 + 1 = 2

Chimps have developed a clever way to collect termites. They poke a stem into a termite nest, then simply withdraw it and lick off the termites.

This veined octopus carries a discarded cockle shell for shelter.

SPECIAL STORAGE
The acorn woodpecker slots acorns and other nuts into purpose-pecked bark cracks, adding more holes each year.

Problem solving

Problem: if you are soft-bodied, how do you guard against hungry enemies? Solution: borrow someone else's protection. The hermit crab uses this technique and will try on several old whelk shells for size to find the best fit. Small fish and octopuses also take advantage of empty seashells as temporary shelters.

Dolphins "talk" using clicks and squeaks as they corral sardines into a baitball, where they can be picked off easily.

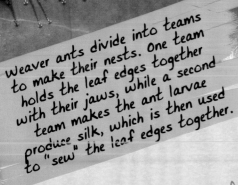

Weaver ants divide into teams to make their nests. One team holds the leaf edges together with their jaws, while a second team makes the ant larvae produce silk, which is then used to "sew" the leaf edges together.

Dream team

Each member of an animal team knows its place and its purpose within the group. Ants are preprogrammed to only follow a few simple instincts, so rarely adapt to new situations. With a decreasing fish population in the oceans, dolphins, however, have developed new methods of finding food—such as chasing trawler nets laden with fish, to feed on any escapees.

abcdef 2×2=4

Strength in NUMBERS

Living and working together in a group can offer some species many advantages. With more animals, there is a greater number of resources—more eyes on the lookout, more defensive weapons to protect the young, and more teeth and claws to attack prey.

Mighty migration

Animals go on annual or seasonal journeys, called migrations, usually due to changes in climate or a seasonal lack of food. Every year, at the start of the wet season (October–November), Christmas Island red crabs move across the shore like an unstoppable red tide, marching into the sea to lay eggs in their millions.

Body building

An inconvenient gap in the path is no problem for a swarming ant colony, especially when they are army ants on the march. The ants simply build a bridge from their own bodies. Neighboring ants lock legs as more climb over them to lengthen the interlinked chains. The bridging ants may stay like this for hours, and even die, as their fellow workers surge over and resume the search for fresh food.

Savage swarms

Locusts require a few months of good conditions to breed and build up their numbers. Gradually, they form an enormous gathering, capable of completely consuming vegetation across an entire region. Continuously in search of fresh greenery, swarms containing hundreds of millions of locusts can quickly ravage farm crops.

Hound dogs

African wild dogs can take down large prey, up to 20 times their own size—using teamwork. The lead dog picks out a young, old, or sick quarry such as a wildebeest. With dogged determination the pack hounds the desperate victim for many miles, until it is so weak from exhaustion that they can move in for the kill.

ANY HINT OF BLOOD IN THE WATER SENDS A GROUP OF RED-BELLIED PIRANHAS INTO A FEEDING FRENZY. WITH DOZENS OF SETS OF RAZOR-SHARP SLASHING TEETH, THEIR FEROCIOUS ATTACK IS IMMEDIATE AND OFTEN FATAL.

Strange Babies

Many animal parents have strong caring instincts, and will even risk their lives to save their babies. Some creatures go to extremes to give their offspring the best chance of survival. The young of some species are born while still at an early stage of development, when they are vulnerable and require constant care. They also look nothing like their parents—in fact, some animal babies look very odd indeed.

▼ A female giant panda gives birth to a single cub, which may stay with her for two years or more. Once a cub is weaned (after the first year), the mother may leave it for days at a time, while she forages for food.

Mini me or metamorphosis?

Some animal offspring, such as seal pups and tiger cubs, are unmistakable mini versions of their parents. Others, such as tadpoles and caterpillars, change dramatically from birth to adulthood. These drastic changes in shape, called metamorphoses, allow the youngsters to live in different environments and eat different foods from the parents, to avoid competing against each other.

Pink and hairless

Many newborn mammals and birds are born when they are still pink and hairless. Their eyes and ears are closed, and they can only feed and sleep. The mother can leave them to find food for herself—once the youngsters are hidden in a nest or a burrow. Her offspring are entirely dependent on her for protection and food.

◄▲ Most caterpillars hatch from eggs a few days after they are laid. They consume vast amounts of leaves before pupating inside a chrysalis and emerging in their adult form to feed on flower nectar.

▼ Seal cubs look just like their parents, except they are born with white fur. They feed on their mother's rich milk and grow faster than any other mammal of their size.

▶ A newborn kangaroo doesn't have proper arms or legs. Yet straight away it has to climb from the birth opening and through its mother's fur to her pouch. Then it attaches to a teat, and stays there for six months until ready to leave the pouch.

Born at an early age

Marsupial mammals such as kangaroos, koalas, wombats, and possums are born at a very early stage of development. Many do not even have recognizable eyes or ears, and their limbs are just flaps or "buds" on the featureless body. These newborns do little except wriggle to the mother's pouch, or marsupium, latch onto a teat with their barely formed mouth, and feed on her milk. Within the protection of the pouch, they continue the stages of development that other mammals go through while still in the womb.

▶ The Virginia opossum may have more tiny pink babies (below) than she has teats. Some die so that the survivors can grow big enough for a ride (above).

Brilliant Builders

Animals create some amazing structures, whether building alone or in groups. Everything they build is for a purpose—a nest to protect their young, a bridge to get from one place to another, or a trap to capture prey. Building methods can vary, depending on what materials are available in a particular habitat.

Supersize it

Some creatures make massive constructions compared to their size. Termites are insects that are only the size of peas, yet their mounds can tower more than 32 ft (10 m) high—that's equivalent to a skyscraper more than 1.5 mi (2.5 km) tall. Other outsizers dig down deep. A network of tunnels built by prairie dogs in Texas, U.S., covered 23,000 sq mi (60,000 sq km) and housed 400 million of these rodents— 20 times more people than in the largest cities.

Actual-size termite

Adult human

20-ft termite mound

◄ Much of the termite mound above the ground is hollow chimneys, made of sun-baked earth. They provide air-conditioning to the main nest below ground level.

◄ The masked weaver tears leaves and stems into strips and delicately intertwines them to create its ball- or flask-shaped nest.

Perfect homemakers

Animals often build nests or burrows to live in for just a short time, usually to raise their young. Most of their behavior is instinctive, but skills and techniques improve greatly with practice. Nests can be made out of a wide range of natural materials, such as grass and mud, as well as materials from other animals, such as feathers and fur.

► The breeding nest of the harvest mouse is hardly larger than a tennis ball. It is built in between stems, high above the ground, to protect the young from danger.

◄▼ A beaver lodge can reach up to 65 ft (20 m) wide and 16 ft (5 m) high.

My home is my castle

The beaver's house, or lodge, is a solid construction of branches, rocks, twigs, and mud. Each generation of beavers carefully fells trees, gnaws off boughs, and adds reinforcements to make an amazing fortress that even hungry wolves and bears cannot break into.

Super STRENGTH

Heavyweight

Elephants can lift logs and other objects weighing up to one ton with their trunks—but the elephant has a great body weight, too, at 5 tons. So a fairer measure of strength is to compare weight moved against body weight—for an elephant, this is just 1/5.

◀ Elephants are the strongest of all land animals, but that's mainly due to their great size.

AN ELEPHANT CAN LIFT ONE FIFTH OF ITS OWN BODY WEIGHT.

Human weightlifters can hoist more than three times their body weight, but that's puny compared to some insects. We are weaklings in other ways too, like our jumping ability, pulling power, or bite strength. But we are champions in one way— as athletic all-rounders.

A WEASEL CAN LIFT 30 TIMES MORE THAN ITS OWN BODY WEIGHT.

Weasels are the world's smallest carnivores, with some individuals weighing little more than one ounce (30 g). They must eat at least one third of their own body weight every day to survive, and can bring down rabbits weighing 35 oz (one kilogram) or more.

A DUNG BEETLE CAN PULL MORE THAN 1,000 TIMES ITS OWN BODY WEIGHT.

ANTS CAN LIFT UP TO 50 TIMES MORE THAN THEIR OWN BODY WEIGHT AND CAN CARRY THE LOAD OVER A DISTANCE OF MANY FEET.

▶ Dung beetles can roll balls of fresh dung up to 30 times more than their own body weight.

Rolling home

Dung beetles roll excrement—from animals including rhinos, wolves, antelopes, elephants, and cats—into balls. While the dung is still moist, the beetles roll the balls to a suitable place, lay eggs inside them, and bury them. The grubs then feed on the dung when they hatch.

A SHARK CAN BITE 60 TIMES HARDER THAN A HUMAN.

Bite size

Bite power depends on whether the biter is angry or relaxed, and whether it uses all its teeth and jaws. Lions, hyenas, sharks, and crocodiles are all super-crunchers, able to crush the bones of prey with ease. However, the extinct dinosaur *T rex* probably had the strongest bite of any animal that has ever lived.

▶ Great white sharks have a strong bite, but the real damage comes from its razor-sharp teeth that can easily saw through flesh and bone.

Can You See Me?

One of the oldest tricks in the animal world is for your body shape, color, pattern, or texture to mimic your surroundings. Camouflage is all about visual trickery and blending in, whether it's to stay unnoticed by enemies or lurk unseen near prey.

A broken-off tree stump merits no second look. Just as well for the great potoo, a night-hunting bird that must stay completely still by day.

Acting the part

Camouflage depends not only on colors, patterns, and shapes, but on movements, too. It's no good merging perfectly into the surroundings, if a sudden movement gives the game away. To be successful, camouflaged creatures must move with extreme care. If the leaf it is resting on blows in the wind, the animal must hang on and sway with it, or risk discovery.

The imperial moth is highly camouflaged on the forest floor, and must rustle and flip with the real leaf litter.

To remain concealed, the leaf-tail gecko must mimic the random motion of a dead leaf—whether remaining motionless or moving with the breeze.

Peering faces

Some predators are not so much well camouflaged as well hidden. Forest frogs, desert toads, and soil-dwelling spiders burrow into the ground, leaving only their eyes and ears exposed to detect passing prey. They must stay like this for hours, until their victim relaxes and strays within reach of their lightning strike.

The Chacoan horned frog almost buries itself in soil, waiting for a beetle or grub to pass by.

A SHARK'S COLORING HELPS IT TO SNEAK UP ON PREY—ITS DARK BACK BLENDS WITH THE SEABED, WHILE ITS PALE BELLY MATCHES THE LIGHTER WATER ABOVE. THIS IS KNOWN AS "COUNTERSHADING."

The nose and eyes of the sidewinding adder match the grains of desert sand around it, hiding it almost completely from view as it waits patiently for its next victim.

Lurking danger

The bigger you are, the more difficult it is to hide from your prey. Big cats have some of the best camouflage colors and patterns, with each species well adapted to its main habitat. Lions are tawny to match the African savanna's dry grasses and dusty soils. Tiger stripes blend in with undergrowth and shrubs, and are particularly effective in the half-light when they are usually out hunting. Leopards and jaguars tend to stay among trees, and their spots mimic the dappled shadows cast by the twigs and leaves above.

A lion peers through the African grassland, perfectly color-matched to its surroundings, on the lookout for food—and danger.

The Big Lineup

Monster creatures are thriving all over the planet. A big animal can usually see off predators easily, and is likely to be strong and able to reach food that others can't. On the downside, these giants have to find and eat lots of food to get the energy they need to survive.

14 ft
13 ft
12 ft
11 ft
10 ft
9 ft
8 ft
7 ft
6 ft
5 ft

BLUE WHALE
Largest animal ever known

105 FT (32 M) Length of its body

198 TONS Weight of its body

3.5 TONS Weight of food it eats in one day

25 FT (7.6 M) Width of its tail

6 TONS Weight of its tongue

30 MPH (48 KM/H) Top swimming speed

1,300 LB (600 KG) Weight of its heart

TALLEST BIRD
Not only is the **OSTRICH** the tallest and heaviest bird, it is also the fastest, reaching a speed of 60 mph (96 km/h). This gigantic bird lays the largest eggs in the world, at 3 lb (1.4 kg) in weight.

LARGEST APE
The large size of the male **GORILLA** allows it to defend its group from attack with intimidating displays involving charging, roaring, and chest beating.

LARGEST MARSUPIAL
Male **RED KANGAROOS** are built for power, with strong tails and sharp claws. When trying to win a female, males can fight or "box" each other, delivering powerful kicks with their muscular hind legs.

OSTRICH
HEIGHT: UP TO 8.8 FT (2.7 M)
WEIGHT: UP TO 310 LB (140 KG)

KODIAK BROWN BEAR
HEIGHT: 7.8 FT (2.4 M)
WEIGHT: UP TO 1,200 LB (545 KG)

RED KANGAROO
HEIGHT: 5.2 FT (1.6 M)
WEIGHT: UP TO 200 LB (90 KG)

GORILLA
HEIGHT: 6 FT (1.8 M)
WEIGHT: UP TO 440 LB (220 KG)

SIBERIAN TIGER
LENGTH: 11 FT (3.3 M) HEAD TO TAIL TIP
WEIGHT: UP TO 660 LB (300 KG)

LARGEST LAND CARNIVORE
The **KODIAK BROWN BEAR** uses its large size to intimidate other large predators. Although battles are rare, its massive strength and size usually results in it winning any violent conflicts.

LARGEST CAT
A powerful, heavily muscled predator, the **SIBERIAN TIGER** uses stalk-and-ambush tactics to bring down large prey, such as deer, single-handedly.

GIRAFFE
HEIGHT: 18 FT (5.5 M)
WEIGHT: 1.4 TONS

14 ft

13 ft

12 ft

11 ft

LARGEST LAND MAMMAL
An angry or frightened **AFRICAN ELEPHANT** can bulldoze anything in its path. A single tusk can reach 10 ft (3 m) long.

ELEPHANT SEAL
LENGTH: 20 FT (6 M)
WEIGHT: 4 TONS

AFRICAN ELEPHANT
HEIGHT: 13 FT (4 M)
WEIGHT: UP TO 6.3 TONS

LARGEST SEAL
A well-fed male **ELEPHANT SEAL** is as heavy as a real elephant. Dominant males, known as "beachmasters," fight fiercely to defend their territories.

TALLEST LAND MAMMAL
The muscular neck of the **GIRAFFE** is as long as a human is tall, and can be swung around like a battering ram to bash predators.

INDEX